The Complete Guides to Horses and Ponies

LEARNING TO RIDE
HORSES&PONIES

Jackie Budd

Gareth Stevens Publishing
MILWAUKEE

For a free color catalog describing Gareth Stevens Publishing's list of high-quality books and multimedia programs, call 1-800-542-2595 (USA) or 1-800-461-9120 (Canada). Gareth Stevens Publishing's Fax: (414) 225-0377. See our catalog, too, on the World Wide Web: http://gsinc.com

Library of Congress Cataloging-in-Publication Data

Budd, Jackie.
[Better riding]
Learning to ride horses and ponies/by Jackie Budd.
p. cm. — (The complete guides to horses and ponies)
Originally published: Better riding.
Lydney, Gloucestershire, England:
Ringpress books, 1996.
Includes index.
Summary: A guide to riding horses and ponies,
discussing such topics as getting started, how
to mount and dismount, sitting right,
riding in a group, and jumping.
ISBN 0-8368-2045-2 (lib. bdg.)
1. Horsemanship—Juvenile literature.
[1. Horsemanship.] I. Title. II. Series: Budd, Jackie.
Complete guides to horses and ponies.
SF309.2.B84   1998
798.2'3—dc21   97-31772

First published in North America in 1998 by
Gareth Stevens Publishing
1555 North RiverCenter Drive, Suite 201
Milwaukee, WI 53212 USA

This U.S. edition © 1998 by Gareth Stevens, Inc.
Created with original © 1996 Ringpress Books Ltd.
and Jackie Budd, P. O. Box 8, Lydney, Gloucestershire,
United Kingdom, GL15 6YD, in association with
Horse & Pony Magazine. All photographs courtesy
of Horse & Pony Magazine. Additional end matter
© 1998 Gareth Stevens, Inc.

The publisher would like to thank Kate Considine,
an experienced rider and trainer, for her assistance
with the accuracy of the text. Ms. Considine
showed in Switzerland for 2-1/2 years and has
worked with Olympians from the USA.
Currently, she is showing and training hunters
and jumpers in the United States.

Printed in Mexico

1 2 3 4 5 6 7 8 9 02 01 00 99 98

CONTENTS

W HEN you begin riding, it is important to learn to do everything as correctly as possible. This is because riding is more than just learning how to stay on a pony and making him go, stop, turn, or jump over a fence.

It is all about learning to communicate with him. Never forget that ponies are a different species from us. They think differently and do not speak our language. Learning to ride involves being able to help a pony understand what you want, and making it easy for him to do it well.

For starters, you need to have a good riding teacher to explain things to you. You also need to learn with the help of cooperative ponies that are likely to do as you ask, if you ask correctly. So, finding a good riding school to get you started is crucial.

Even when you think you have the hang of riding — and perhaps have a pony of your own — the very best riders will always tell you that you never stop learning. Take regular lessons from a professional instructor to make sure no bad habits are creeping in, or to help iron out any riding problems that might arise.

EVEN if you ride only once a week, spend the days in between finding out all you can about horses and ponies. Learn about the different parts of the horse and the saddlery — it will come in handy for lessons. Helping at the stables is a great way of gaining experience. And never be afraid to ask questions!

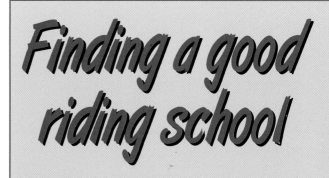

Getting

Finding a good riding school

Y OU or your parents may not have had much to do with horses before, but it is not hard to tell a good place to learn to ride from a bad one. Whether the school you plan to use is large or small, here are a few pointers:

◆ A FRIENDLY WELCOME: **Well-run schools have cheerful, polite staff members who are happy to help you.**

◆ A NEAT YARD: **Even if it is not all brand new, the yard and tack room should be tidy with clean, roomy stables kept in good repair. There should be**

Horses should look clean and alert.

The correct gear ...

FOR your first lessons, there is no need to buy a lot of expensive gear, as long as you are wearing comfortable and practical clothes. Two important items you will need are boots and a riding hat.

Hat You must wear a riding helmet that meets the latest approved safety standards. In the United States, the Troxel line of hats is rated the best. Some schools lend or rent hats, but it is better to buy one fitted properly just for you. If a hat does not fit well, it will not give much protection — it must sit well down on the head, not tip back or forward, and be snug but not tight. The "jockey skull" type hats *(right)* have a velvet cover.

started

Welcome aboard: look for a well-run school with a cheerful staff when you sign up for lessons.

plenty of pastures, safe fencing, and a tidy manure heap away from the stables.

◆ HAPPY HORSES: **Make sure the ponies look content, well-fed, clean, and alert. Check that their feet are in good condition with no sore spots.**

◆ SAFETY FIRST: **Riders should all be wearing up-to-date helmets. Ponies should be well behaved and suitable for their riders. In the yard, tools should be put away and first-aid and fire equipment close at hand, with "No Smoking" a strict rule.**

◆ LESSON TIME: **Watch a lesson *(right)* to see if everyone seems to be having a good time and learning, too. Classes should have no more than six pupils.**

◆ FACILITIES: **It helps if the school has an all-weather outdoor ring, or, better still, an indoor arena.**

Boots
Any sturdy shoes or boots will do for starters, as long as they have a small heel and no buckles. Rain boots are not safe because the soles can easily get stuck in the stirrups — nor are tennis shoes. Proper riding boots, either long rubber ones or short paddock boots, are not too expensive.

Other equipment for comfort and safety:

BRITCHES:
  Close-fitting trousers.
GLOVES:
  To protect your hands.
BODY PROTECTOR:
  A padded coat that will help absorb the impact in case you fall off.

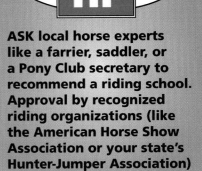

TIP

ASK local horse experts like a farrier, saddler, or a Pony Club secretary to recommend a riding school. Approval by recognized riding organizations (like the American Horse Show Association or your state's Hunter-Jumper Association) will guarantee standards.

Your first

A T your first lesson, the instructor will probably explain some basic things to you about the pony you will be riding and the tack the pony is wearing. The instructor will have chosen a pony that is the right size for you, is used to beginners, and is well-mannered.

It will all seem pretty strange at first. If you have never ridden before, just the movement of the pony's walk might seem uncomfortable and fast-moving.

But don't worry — with the help of your teacher, you will soon be feeling confident and in control.

LISTEN FOR THE BASICS

Lunge lessons

Y OU might start with a few individual lessons on the lunge. This is where the instructor stands in the middle of the arena, and the pony circles around her on the end of a long rein called a lunge line.

Lunge lessons help you learn quickly because you can focus on the way you are sitting. You can relax knowing that the instructor has control of where the pony is going, and how fast. Lessons on the lunge are good for all riders because they help improve your "seat" (the way you are sitting in the saddle) and teach you to keep your balance.

YOU may be offered either private lessons or class lessons, where you will be learning in a group. Class lessons are less expensive and perhaps more fun because you have the company of others. You can also learn from watching others. At the start of your lessons, however, it is worth paying a little extra for a few individual lessons. Whichever you choose, the instructor will probably start off by leading you or having a helper lead you on the pony, just until you feel confident and have learned the right signals to tell the pony what to do. These signals are called the aids.

MANY ponies blow their tummies out when the saddle is first put on. This means that, when you mount, the girth (the strap that fastens the saddle on the pony) is far too loose. If you tried to get on at this point, you would probably end up underneath rather than on top of the pony! So, first lift up the saddle flap and tighten both of the buckles of the girth, so the saddle will not slip around. Walk around the front of the pony and check that the buckles are level there. Once the girth is tight, pull each of the forelegs forward to even out any wrinkles in the skin.

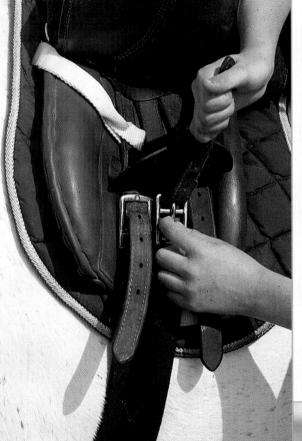

Things to check before you climb on board

NOW pull the stirrup irons down the back of the leathers to the bottom. Standing alongside the pony, facing the saddle, check that the stirrups will be about the right length for you. Do this by clenching your fist and holding it up against the stirrup bar (where the leathers attach to the saddle). The iron should just about reach your armpit. If nobody is holding your pony for you, always have an arm looped through the reins while you are doing these checks. Never leave the pony standing loose.

Mounting

GETTING up into the saddle is called mounting, and this is one of the first things you will learn at your riding school. Mounting the right way is important for your safety, but also to make the process comfortable for the pony.

When you are first learning to mount, your instructor or a helper will probably hold the pony to make sure the pony stands still. If you are getting on from the ground, it is also helpful to have someone pulling down on the stirrup iron on the far side of the saddle to keep the saddle from moving around on the pony's back.

Usually, a pony is mounted from his near or left-hand side.

How to get on board . . .

Step by Step

1 STAND on the pony's near side with your left shoulder alongside his shoulder, facing toward his tail. Gather up the reins so they are short but not tight, to stop the pony from moving. Putting both reins into the left hand, place your hand on the pony's mane just above the withers. The spare ends of the reins need to be dropped over the other side of the pony's neck, out of the way. If you have a whip, hold it in your left hand, so it doesn't go all over.

2 TAKE the stirrup iron in your right hand, bringing the far side toward you — this will make sure the leather lies flat under your leg once you are on. Keeping your weight forward, put your left foot well into the stirrup, so the ball of the foot is on the iron. Now hop around so you are facing the pony's side, pressing down into the stirrup as much as you can so your toe goes under the belly instead of poking into it. Your right hand goes either on the pony's withers, perhaps grasping a bit of mane, on the pommel (front) of the saddle, or, if you can reach, over the far side of the saddle at the waist (middle section). Never hang onto the cantle (back), as this can twist and damage the saddle.

hints

...and how not to do it!

3 NOW push up with your right foot with as much spring as you can. Straighten your left knee so you are standing in the stirrup, and swing your right leg well clear over the pony's back. Your right hand now needs to move to the pommel of the saddle.

3

4 AS your leg swings over, turn your body to face forward and lower yourself gently into the saddle. Do not come down with a thump! Without letting go of the reins, see if you can feel for the other stirrup and put your right foot in it. At first, you may need to look down and check where it is and to make sure the leather is not twisted. Then, take the reins in both hands. With just one or two adjustments, you are ready to go.

4

WHOOPS! You can tell by the expression on this pony's face *(above)* that he does not like having the rider's toe digging into his ribs. Keep your toe down as you pivot around. Your pony could easily mistake a nudge in the side as a signal to walk on — the last thing you want when you're trying to mount!

OUCH! Dragging your right leg across the pony's quarters *(below)* is a sure way to make him jump forward in surprise. Lift your leg clear — and pick up those reins, too!

Mounting

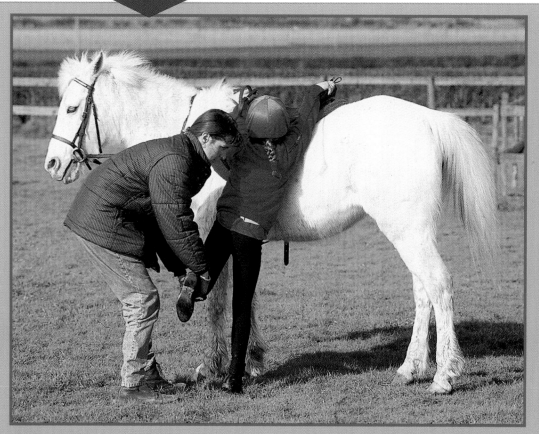

HAVING A LEG-UP

THIS is especially useful for a small person getting on a big horse! Grasp the reins in your left hand, and stand facing the pony's near side. Put your right hand over the saddle. Now bend your left knee up so your helper can hold it.

Count: "One, two..." and, on the "three," your helper pushes you up at the same time that you spring off your right foot. As you go up, swing your leg well clear over the pony's back, and land lightly in the saddle. It is better to hold the far side of the saddle rather than the cantle, as shown here.

VAULTING ON

THIS is for the real experts (on small ponies). With your left hand holding the reins on the withers and your right hand reaching over the seat of the saddle, bend your knees and spring up. You need to push down on your arms until your body is well over the pony's back, high enough to swing your leg over the saddle.

USING A MOUNTING BLOCK *(above)*

THIS is handy if the saddle is a long way up! It also puts less strain on the pony's back than the ordinary way of mounting. If you have access to a mounting block, it's worth using. Position the pony alongside the block with the saddle nearest the block. Grasp the reins in your left hand, and stand on the block. Put your left foot in the stirrup. With your right hand over the saddle, get on and settle down lightly.

hints 2

WHOA! Before you can move off, there are just a couple more checks to make sure that the saddle is secured in the correct position and your stirrups are at the right length for your legs. If you have ever ridden in a slipping saddle, you will know how dangerous this can be. And stirrups that are too long or short mean you will not be able to balance properly or use your legs very effectively. So it is important to get these things right at the start.

ADJUSTING THE STIRRUPS

TAKE your feet out of the stirrups, and let your feet dangle. For the stirrups to be a suitable length, the bottom of the irons should be just about the same level as your ankles. If they are too long or short, you will need to put the reins into one hand. With your foot in the iron, move your thigh back a bit and find the stirrup leather buckle under the skirt of the saddle.

PULL the buckle up, move the prong to the appropriate hole, and pull down on the inside of the leather so the buckle slots back into place at the top. At first, you will probably find you need your instructor's help. But with practice, you'll soon be able to do this without even looking down.

TIGHTENING THE GIRTH

SETTLE down into the saddle. If no one is holding your pony, make sure your reins are short enough to stop him from moving off. Now take both reins into your right hand, laying the left rein flat against the right one across your palm. Without taking your foot out of the stirrup, bring your left leg forward past the front knee roll of the saddle.

WITH your free hand, lift the saddle flap so you can see the girth straps. Look down, and, holding the ends of the straps firmly, pull up each one in turn and tighten it as much as you can. When the buckles are in place, put the flap down and slide your leg back in place.

TIP Whichever way you get on, always make sure your pony stands still until you have made all your adjustments. Letting him wander off before you are ready is a bad habit.

G ETTING off the pony is called dismounting. There is a right and wrong way to do it. When you first begin riding, dismounting from even a small pony seems a long way down. But before long, you will be leaping off all sizes of horses and ponies easily.

Dismounting

M AKE sure your pony is standing still. Take both feet out of the stirrups and hold both reins in your left hand. If you are carrying a whip, make sure this is also in your left hand, or it might fly around as you dismount. Put your right hand on the front of the saddle and lean forward.

The right way to dismount

S WING your right leg clear of the pony's back and drop down as lightly as you can, bending your knees slightly as you reach the ground. You need to finish up next to your pony's shoulder on his near (left) side. Never try to dismount by flinging your leg over the pony's withers in front of you. Dropping the reins will mean you have no control. And if your pony is frightened by seeing your leg swing up, and he moves forward, you could fall off backward onto your head — ouch!

hints

TIP

RIDERS in some stables are taught to dismount leaving their left foot in the stirrup and stepping down. But take care not to poke your toe into the pony's side as you swing around or he might move off unexpectedly.

Step by Step

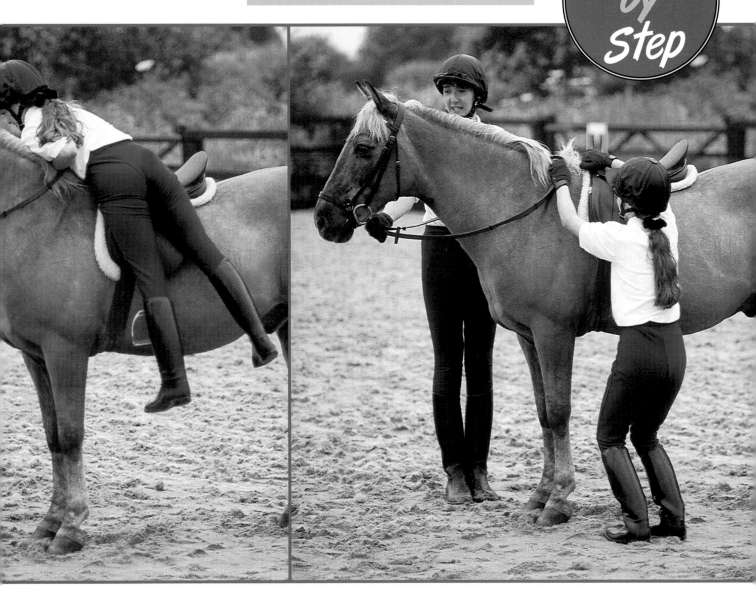

AFTER you have dismounted, there are a few things to do to make your pony safe and comfortable.

RUN UP THE STIRRUPS:

THIS stops the stirrups from banging against the pony's sides and catching on something as you lead him. Take each stirrup iron and push it up the back of the leather to the top near the buckle. Tuck the end of the leather through the iron.

LOOSENING THE GIRTH:

ALLOW your pony to breathe out and relax after all his hard work by loosening his girth a little. Once the stirrups have been run up, lift up the near-side saddle flap and release the girth strap just one or two holes. If your pony is wearing a bridle with a drop-type noseband (one that fits *below* the bit), it is kind to loosen this slightly as well.

THE reins are one method the rider has of communicating with the pony — or giving the signals known as aids. Along with aids from your legs, the reins can be used to ask the pony to slow down, to move more briskly instead of poking along, and to turn or bend his body to one side or the other.

As soon as you mount, quickly take the reins and adjust their length so you have control. There is a particular way to hold the reins and position your hands for the best results. Then you will be able to easily give your rein aids and allow your pony to understand the slightest signal.

Taking up

Holding the reins

THE rein comes from the bit and passes between your little and third fingers, goes up through your palm, and comes out between your first finger and your thumb for a firm hold.

Adjusting the reins

HOLD the rein buckle in your left hand. With your right hand, grasp the right rein farther down nearer the bit. Hold it as pictured *(above)*. Use your right thumb and forefinger to take hold of the left rein, freeing your left hand. Now take the left rein into the left hand at the same length as the other side. If you want to shorten the length of both reins, do this, one at a time, by using the opposite hand to draw the rein through each hand. Shorten the reins in this way whenever you feel they are getting long. You do not need to halt — you can do this as you move along. The reins should always be the same length and never be twisted.

Where the hands go

WHENEVER you are riding, at whatever speed, your hands must stay level with each other just above the pony's withers — about 4 inches (10 centimeters) apart. If you keep knocking your hands on the front of the saddle, or if you get greasy gloves or knuckles from rubbing on the pony's coat, your hands are too low.

the reins

Bad hand positions

WHEN you are holding the reins correctly, you can signal down them just by squeezing your fingers, hardly moving your hand at all. There should be no need to pull or tug with a backward movement. But you must keep your thumbs on top all the time — then they can keep a grip on the reins while your other fingers do the squeezing. In this way, your entire hand and wrist stay relaxed, and you can have a sensitive feel on the pony's mouth.

If you turn your wrists over so the knuckles are on top or your wrists are bent in *(above)*, you lose that direct line to the pony's mouth. In addition, your wrist will stiffen. The same

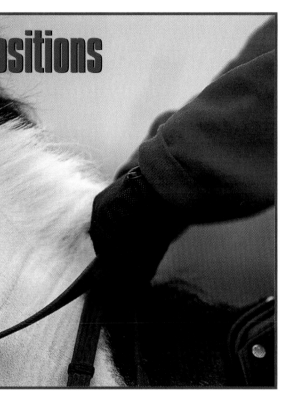

goes for sticking your thumbs out so your palms are upward. Always keep your thumbnails on top.

It takes time to learn to keep your hands steady. At first, you will probably find your instructor reminds you often.

Contact: The "feel" down the reins . . .

YOU will hear your instructor talking about having the right contact with the reins. This means the "feel" or pressure that you have on the pony's mouth.

The reins should never be used for hanging onto the pony or getting your balance. Ponies' mouths are very sensitive, so never be rough with the reins or yank on them to tell a pony "no." However, you do need to have a feel of the pony's mouth or you won't be able to tell him what to do. There is no point in having your reins too long

or loose. But you do not want them to be too short and tight either, or he will be uncomfortable. Getting and keeping the correct pressure on the reins might take a while to get used to. Once you achieve a good contact, try to keep that feel all the time by making adjustments when the pony's head position changes.

Keep them level

TRY not to have one hand higher than the other because your pony will get different messages from each one. Never let them cross over the pony's neck — keep them on either side of the withers, even when you are turning a corner.

Sitting right

HANGING on by the reins is not the way to stay on a pony, and neither is gripping as tightly as you can with your legs. Your aim is to stay on the pony simply by sitting upright, in balance, on the pony's back. That means sitting in the right position and keeping in it, no matter what the pony is doing.

The right position does more than just keep you on board and in balance. It keeps your legs and hands in exactly the right place to give the aids and send clear messages to your pony. It might feel awkward at first, so you have to concentrate hard to stay there. But as you get better and better, you will find you can keep your position without thinking about it — kind of like riding a bike.

RELAX! It is very important to stay relaxed when you are in the saddle. If you are tense, you will not be able to give the aids properly. Your pony will sense right away that you are nervous and get worried himself. So, don't try too hard. Take a few deep breaths, and try to sit as naturally (but not sloppily) as you can.

KEEP your head up and look between the pony's ears *(inset, top).* Do not look sideways or down. Try to sit up straight, without tensing your shoulders. Think about keeping your shoulders level, not dipping one down to the side. Hold your hands level just above the withers. You are aiming for a straight line from the bit, along the reins, through your wrists to your elbows.

The correct position . . .

SIT down deep in the very center of the saddle. Try not to lean to one side, or you will not be in balance. Sit squarely with your weight evenly spread over both of your seat-bones.

and how not to do it!

THIS rider is sitting too stiffly, with a hollow back and tense body. She needs to bring her hands down and elbows back to get a softer contact with the pony's mouth. To give her pony a leg aid, she would have to swing her entire leg back — with toes stuck out as pictured. She is sure to bang her heels into the pony's sides and give him a surprising shock!

LET your legs hang loosely down over the saddle flaps. Your foot is positioned with the stirrup alongside the girth, so the knee and toe are in line. The ball of the foot is on the stirrup iron, with a little weight in the iron so the toes are slightly up and the heel slightly down. The toes must point straight ahead. You should be able to draw an imaginary line through the head, shoulders, elbows, and hips, right down to your heels. Your instructor will help adjust your position until you know what feels right.

AT last we are about to get moving! It is time to learn the aids — the instructions you use to tell the pony what you want him to do. Expert riders can give many different variations on the aids to ask a well-trained horse or pony to do quite complicated movements. But, for now, all you need to know is how to tell the pony to move forward, slow down or stop, and make simple turns. A combination of signals from your legs and hands accomplishes these movements. The other natural aids are the voice and seat.

The aids and their uses . . .

LEGS
Your legs ask the pony to move forward faster. They also help keep him straight or turn him.

HANDS
Your hands, on the reins, help control your pony's speed and the direction he is going.

VOICE
Your voice can be useful, at times, to help encourage a pony, soothe him, or praise him. But don't overdo it or keep chatting to your pony constantly.

SEAT
Advanced riders, who are very secure in the saddle, can use their back and seat muscles, together with their leg aids, to help balance the horse and make him move more actively. This is something you will learn as your riding improves. For now, just concentrate on staying in a good position in the saddle. But always remember that any change in your body position shifts your weight on the pony and will affect his balance.

Steady as you go

ONCE your pony is going forward at the speed you want, hold your legs still, as relaxed as you can, close to his sides just behind the girth. As the pony walks, think about keeping that great position you had when he was standing still. As you feel the pony's head move forward and back a little as he walks, you should allow your hands to follow that movement.

◆ KEEP the contact on the reins steady — just ease them back and forward, but don't jerk them.

◆ TRY to sit up straight with your shoulders back. Keep the top half of your body as still as you can.

◆ DON'T grip with your lower legs, just let them hang loosely close to the pony's sides. Once you are moving, keep your lower legs still.

ARTIFICIAL AIDS

YOU may find it useful to carry a whip, which is known as an "artificial" aid, to back up your legs in case your pony does not respond to them. The whip is usually carried in the hand nearest the center of the arena (the inside hand). It fits through the palm and lies across the thigh, not down the pony's shoulder or waving around in the air.

move

Transitions

YOU will need to use the aids whenever you want to make a transition — that is, to change the pace, or speed, at which your pony is moving. When you ask your pony to go up a pace, this is called an upward transition. Asking him to move into a slower pace is called a downward transition. Whether you are increasing speed or decreasing it, the aids for going faster are always the same, and the aids for going slower are always the same.

The difficult part is to stay in position and give the aids consistently, so that your pony understands them.

From halt to walk

GET into a good position on your pony. Sit up straight with your rear end down in the saddle. Now close the lower part of your legs around the pony's sides just behind the girth.

As you squeeze, keep your heels down in the stirrups, like in the *(top)* picture, moving your legs inward and only slightly back.

If you kick upward like the picture *(bottom)*, your leg tenses up, and your body has to tip forward, throwing you and the pony off balance. The aim is to be able to give each aid without having to move any other part of your body.

As the pony starts to move forward, let your hands release the contact a little by easing slightly forward. Now the pony knows he is supposed to be moving on, so you can stop the leg aid. If you get your aids right and your pony is well trained, he should respond right away. If he does not, maybe he didn't "hear" you. So check your position and try again, a bit more firmly, and he should respond. You will soon learn to judge how much pressure you need.

As you get better at giving the aids, in time, they will be almost invisible to anyone watching.

Walking

NOW you are sitting correctly in the saddle, and it is time to think about walking on. This sounds simple enough — after all, the pony is doing all the work! However, it is important that you also play your part. Your pony must walk on actively and with energy, and you must steer him in the direction you want to go. Can you feel the four-time beat of the walk? It goes one – two – three – four. Aim to get your pony walking in a straight line, with a regular beat.

Three ways not to walk

COME on, don't let him go to sleep! If your pony won't walk or is dragging his feet, check to see that your reins are short enough and use your legs again to hurry him up.

HINTS ON SLOWING DOWN

BEFORE going any farther, let's learn how to stop and steer.

Walk to halt

WHEN you want to slow down or halt, sit as upright as you can. Press your rear end down into the saddle. Keep your legs close to the pony's sides.

With a responsive pony, there should be no need to pull on the reins. Just keep your hands still, so the pony feels a resistance and knows you want to go slower. Some ponies may need just a squeeze on the reins before they get the message, but never tug or pull back on the reins. As soon as your pony responds, ease the pressure off so he knows he has done what you wanted.

THE rider (*above*) needs a few more lessons. You should always keep your lower legs underneath you and close to the pony's sides. To give a leg aid, this rider will have to move her entire leg backward. Look how her leg position has shifted all her weight to the back of the saddle, making her completely out of balance.

YOU can see this pony does not like the leg flapping going on in the picture on the *right*.

About

AS long as you are sitting squarely in the center of the saddle, and you are using both your legs at the same place on each side of your pony, he should walk straight ahead. When you want to make a turn, each leg and hand has a different job.

To turn, your inside hand (the one toward the inside of the ring, on the side you are turning) squeezes the rein gently, making the pony turn his head and neck slightly to guide him in the direction you want to turn.

Your outside hand (the one on the outside of the ring) is allowed to move forward slightly as the pony begins to turn his head. Both hands should stay level. Keep an even contact on the reins throughout the turn.

Do not release the outside hand too much or the pony's head will bend too much into the turn, and he might go too fast. Use this hand to control the pony's speed, too. Your inside leg is pressing inward into the pony's side, by the girth. This tells the pony to keep moving forward. Think of the turn as bending the pony's body around this leg.

Your outside leg is the one that is helping the pony turn. Use it just behind the girth to stop the pony's quarters from swinging out and to keep his body bending around the curve.

turns

X

X

"Do"s and "Don't"s

DO turn your head slightly to look in the direction you are going. This helps because it turns your shoulders and hips a little that way, too, so these stay in line with the pony's shoulders during the turn. The tiny change in your balance helps your pony bend through the turn. But don't strain to look — stay sitting up straight.

DO think about your turn in plenty of time, so you don't take your pony by surprise. Try to make your turn a nice, even bend, not a sharp corner that throws you out of balance.

DON'T let your pony grind to a halt. Keep him moving forward in an active, even rhythm throughout the turn.

DON'T lean inward *(above, right)*, drop your inside shoulder down, or slide your rear end out. Sit as upright and square as you can.

DON'T pull your pony around with the rein only *(above, left)* or use too much rein and hardly any leg. You may end up turning his head and neck, but the rest of him will keep going straight! Aim to get his whole body bending in the direction you are turning. To do this, you hardly need any pressure — just a combination of "feel" on the inside rein, "give" on the outside rein, and "feel" with the outside leg.

Trotting:

WALK is a steady pace that you will soon get the hang of. Moving up a gear to trot could take a little longer to get used to. In a trot, you will probably feel you are going quite a lot faster. At first, be prepared for a bumpy ride until you've mastered the skill of posting trot. Trot is much bouncier than walk because, in trot, the pony moves in a one-two rhythm, springing from one diagonal pair of feet to the other diagonal pair, with a brief moment in between each spring when all his feet are off the ground.

Posting trot

WHEN you begin riding, you will be taught posting trot — which means learning to lift your seat a little out of the saddle with the trot's "up" beat and sitting gently back in the saddle for the "down" beat. This makes things easier on the pony's back and on your rear end!

Posting to the trot takes practice, so don't expect to grasp it immediately. Try it in halt first, concentrating on keeping your legs in the right place, body upright, and hands still, while your body moves slightly up and down. The first time your pony trots, you will probably tense up and tip forward and have to grab at something (make this the mane or neckstrap, not the reins). But try to relax, and keep your head and body up. Count the one-two rhythm out loud.

Let yourself be pushed up by the upbeat, your body coming slightly forward, then back down into the saddle with the downbeat.

Concentrate on letting your weight sink down through your heels. Keep practicing and, all of a sudden, you will click into time with the movement — and away you'll go!

TIP

LOTS of riders try too hard with their posting trot *(right)*, standing up in the stirrups so they have a long way to come down again with each beat. Try to relax, and just let the swinging movement of the trot lift you a little way up out of the saddle. Think about simply pushing your hips forward with each beat.

basics

TIP

WHAT if you are on a slow-moving horse? Having to kick him to keep him moving on in trot throws you out of position when you are trying to do posting trot as well. First, check that you have your reins short enough and that you are not tipping forward. Now use your whip to give him a quick smack behind the girth to encourage him. Do this immediately whenever you feel him fading.

From walk to trot

THE aids for moving from walk into trot are exactly the same as halt to walk, except that you may have to use them more firmly. First, make sure your pony is awake and walking with a spring in his step. Check that your reins have a good contact.

Now sit up, press your rear end down into the saddle, and squeeze (or nudge inward, if necessary) with both legs on the pony's sides. Remember that, as you ask with your legs, you have to allow a little with your hands so he knows it's OK to move onward.

Once the pony is trotting, don't start posting immediately. Sit for a few trot beats to help your balance until he is going in a good rhythm. You don't need to keep using your leg aids once the pony is trotting. Only use them again if you feel him slowing down, or want to trot faster.

WHENEVER you want your pony to move up a pace, sit up as straight as you can, and keep your reins short and your legs in the right place. Otherwise, he does not know what is going on.

Trotting:

Whoops!

1 NO prizes for guessing what is going wrong here (1). Hands stuck out, legs forward and far from the pony's sides, weight thumping on the back of the saddle — no wonder this pony is not enjoying himself.

2 DON'T panic! This rider (2) is flustered, and everything is going wrong. She's hanging onto the reins and gripping as hard as she can with her knees, so her heels have come up, throwing her forward. Her pony thinks her legs are saying "Go!" and is worried and confused about why she is pulling on his mouth. She needs to slow down to walk, get organized, and try again. Shortening the stirrups a little will help her keep a better position.

3 CAN you see how, by falling forward (3), the reins have become too long, the rider's legs have moved too far back, and all the pony's weight has been thrown onto his front end? She would have a lot more success by sitting up in balance, shortening the reins, and driving him on so his hindquarters produce more active steps.

2

It's all in the balance!

REMEMBER that, at whatever pace your pony is moving, you are trying to keep the balanced position you were in when he was standing still — despite all the bouncing up and down. Although your body inclines forward a little as you post to the trot, this should not tip your weight onto the pony's front end.

KEEP looking up between the pony's ears all the time. Your hands should be level — but unlike in walk when they "give" with the pony's head movement, in trot, they stay still. Your legs need to keep still, too, even though you are rising up and down. They must stay snugly closed around the pony's sides without gripping (don't let your heel creep up) or shooting backward and forward as you rise and fall.

From trot to walk

TO slow down from trot to walk, first stop posting for a few beats. Sit as tall as you can, and keep your lower leg underneath you, closed around the pony's sides. Brace your back, press your rear end down into the saddle, and gently put pressure on the reins. Don't pull on the reins unless your pony takes no notice. As he eases into walk, release the pressure and allow your hands to move with his head. These riders are having trouble coming down to walk because they are tense and have forgotten to sit upright. The one on the *left* has tipped forward so far that she is looking down and her rear end is out of the saddle. Her hands are pulling and set too low. Her leg is gripping with the knee and heel, giving her horse all the wrong signals. She needs to relax and sit tall. The rider on the *right* is trying to slow down by pulling on the reins. Because her leg has slipped back, her pony thinks he is supposed to be going faster. She must loosen her shoulders, push her heels down, relax her arms, and use on-off, give-and-take squeezes on the reins to slow the pony down.

Sitting trot

IT is possible not to post to the trot but to stay sitting in the saddle all the time. You will see expert riders using sitting trot a lot because when you can do it well, it gives you much more control over the horse and his balance.

To sit to the trot without being tossed around, keep upright and stay very relaxed in your body and legs so that all the bounce is absorbed by your limber knees and hips. Sounds hard? Well, it does take a little practice, and it is tiring at first. But as long as you don't tip forward or grip with your legs, you will find that staying in position by just using your balance is not as difficult as you would expect. This is what you are aiming for in all your riding — staying in balance with your pony all the time, no matter what he is

doing. So practicing sitting trot is a great way to help you develop what is called an independent seat — that is, to sit deep and square in the saddle and to stay there without relying on the reins or stirrups. It is worth trying to improve your sitting trot — don't forget, you actually need to sit for a few beats when you prepare to make a transition in or out of trot — and it will be especially useful when you canter. The better you are sitting, the better your transitions will be.

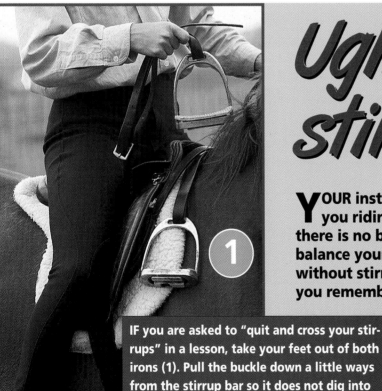

(1)

IF you are asked to "quit and cross your stirrups" in a lesson, take your feet out of both irons (1). Pull the buckle down a little ways from the stirrup bar so it does not dig into your thigh. Now take the right leather over the front of the saddle first, then the left. The left is last, so if you get off and want to mount again, the near-side stirrup is easy to take back.

Ugh – no stirrups

YOUR instructor is interested in getting you riding without stirrups because there is no better way to help you learn to balance yourself. Of course, sitting trot without stirrups is incredibly bumpy. So, do you remember what you need to do to stay on board and even keep smiling? Sit up, look up, legs long, and relax! If you do feel yourself tipping to one side, do not grab the reins. Grab some mane or the neckstrap and think "shoulders back, legs underneath" to get yourself upright again. Don't worry, though,

3

WHEN you are in trot, you need to learn about diagonals. When a pony trots, he springs from one pair of legs to the other. In posting trot, the rider rises and falls to this beat.

As you start doing different exercises and movements in the ring, it becomes more important to sit and rise to the correct beat for two reasons:

◆ IF you were to always rise to one particular pair of legs and sit to the other, the pony would soon become stiff and one-sided.

◆ WHEN you are moving around a circle, the pony will be better balanced if you sit as his outside shoulder moves backward. So, if you are

Diagonal thinking

going around to the right (on the right rein), you sit as the left shoulder comes back — this is the pony's left diagonal. Going around on the left rein, you sit as the right shoulder comes back — the pony's right diagonal.

Experienced riders learn to tell which diagonal they are sitting on just by feel. But at first, you'll need to glance down (don't lean over) to see which shoulder is moving back as you sit.

Making a change

YOU will have to change diagonal every time you change direction, so that you always stay on the correct (outside) one.

It's simple — all you do is sit down for an extra beat. So instead of going "up-down-up-down," you go "up-down-down-up." Glance down now, and you will see you have changed diagonal.

The rider pictured (*above*) is going around on the right rein and is on the "down" beat of the trot. Is she on the correct diagonal? (*Answer below*).

your instructor should not ask you to trot without stirrups until you have gotten very good at trotting with them.

Although the rider in picture 3 is leaning back a little, her legs are hanging down loose and she looks much more secure than the rider in picture 2.

Most riders make their first attempt without stirrups on a lunge, as pictured, so they don't have to worry about controlling the pony.

ANSWER: No, she should be sitting as the outside shoulder comes back, not the inside one.

Riding in

IT'S one thing having control over your pony when you are riding on your own or in an individual lesson. But when you join a group of other riders, you will really need to concentrate. There is not only your riding style and your own pony to think about — you have to watch where everyone else is going and make sure you don't get in their way.

MOST group lessons take place in an enclosed arena or indoor ring. As part of a group of students, you will need to learn certain instructions and terms the instructor uses to keep all the riders organized. There are also some safety rules designed to avoid collisions and other accidents.

YOU could find the quiet pony you have been used to is quite a different character when he gets in a group. Most ponies are livelier in a group lesson and may try to confuse things by cutting corners, trying to drift toward the others, being reluctant to leave new friends to work on their own, or putting on an extra burst of speed to catch up with the rest of the pack!

BE prepared for your pony to spook if another one comes close behind or next to him, and always think and look ahead. Be sure to be considerate and aware of other riders.

TIP

ALWAYS listen carefully to what your instructor says. When you have a chance, watch the others, too. You can learn a lot from any and all of the instructor's comments. And don't be afraid to ask questions if there is anything you are not sure about.

Language lesson

RIDE: Name for a group of riders. In most lessons, the ride will follow in a single file.

LEFT REIN: Going around to the left.

RIGHT REIN: Going around to the right.

CHANGE THE REIN: Moving across the ring and turning the other way when you reach the other side, so you are going the opposite way around the ring.

OUTSIDE TRACK: The path around the edge of the ring.

INSIDE TRACK: A path around the ring, 10 feet (3 meters) inward from the outside track.

CENTER LINE: An imaginary line down the center of the ring lengthways.

"PREPARE TO": An introductory way for your instructor to warn you when she is about to tell you to move up a pace or slow down to prepare for a transition.

a group

KEEP YOUR DISTANCE

When you are riding in single file, don't let your pony have his nose right up to the tail of the pony in front. This is asking to get kicked. Keep a distance of at least one pony's length between you and the rider ahead. If you are lagging behind, hurry your pony along to close up the gap. If your pony's pace is faster than the one ahead, it is OK to circle away and join in somewhere else. Just be sure you look ahead and plan where you are going.

SLOWING DOWN AND STOPPING

Before slowing down, think first in case there is someone right behind you, or you may cause a pile-up! If you want to go down a pace from the rest of the group, move to the inside track out of the way. Go to the center of the ring if you need to adjust your girth or stirrups *(right)*.

Stick to the rules

PASSING

Whenever passing another rider, don't get too close. Allow at least a pony's width between. If you are traveling in opposite directions, keep a lookout for other riders approaching and always stay to the right. Usually, students have the right of way over other riders.

ASK FIRST

Whenever you are coming into or leaving a ring where riders are working, get permission from your instructor to proceed. Then make sure the way is clear.

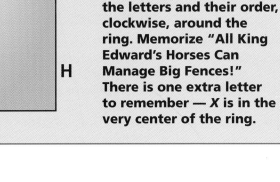

The ring

MOST rings have markers around the outside with the letters *A, K, E, H, C, M, B,* and *F*. Try to learn these because your instructor will use them when she gives commands. There is an easy way to remember the letters and their order, clockwise, around the ring. Memorize "All King Edward's Horses Can Manage Big Fences!" There is one extra letter to remember — *X* is in the very center of the ring.

A
F   K
B   X   E
M   H
C

DURING your lesson, the instructor will ask the entire group, or each rider individually, to do ring movements or exercises. These include various turns, circles, and loops that help you practice your riding skills. As you become a better rider, you can also use these exercises to help your pony become more limber and obedient — this is known as "schooling" your pony. Listen carefully to your instructor because she will tell you at which marker you should start and finish each movement. Here are some of the movements you are likely to come across, and what your goals are:

LARGE 65-FOOT (20-M) CIRCLES

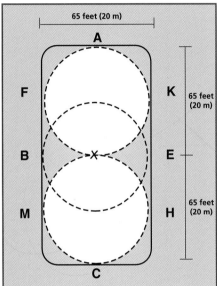

HALF 65-FOOT (20-M) CIRCLES

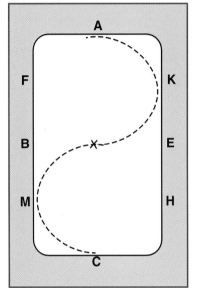

SMALL 32-FOOT (10-M) CIRCLES

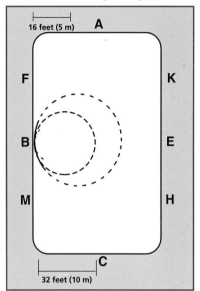

Circles

WHERE YOU GO: A large circle (65 feet or 20 meters) takes up all of one end of the ring, touching each side and the *X* in the center *(above, left)*. You could also start a large circle at *B* or *E*. Smaller circles are 32-50 feet or 10-15 m across *(above, right)*. A 32-foot (10-m) circle reaches the center line. You may also be asked to do a half-circle, changing the rein when you get halfway so that the movement forms an *S*-shape *(above, center)*.

YOUR AIM: To make an even-shaped, accurate circle. To get your pony's entire body bending around a circle by using your hand and leg aids.

Figure eight

WHERE YOU GO: In figure eight, leave the track just after a corner marker. Head diagonally across the ring, passing through *X* — this is called going "across the diagonal." Continue around the end of the ring. Then at the corner marker, start across the diagonal again to the far side corner marker where you started.

YOUR AIM: To make your pony leave the track when he is asked. To keep him straight across the diagonal and exactly reach the marker at the other side. To make a nice bend around the short end of the ring, then do the same going the other way. It should all be done in one flowing movement with no sharp corners or changes of speed.

movements

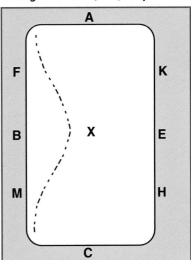

Riding a 16-foot (5-m) loop

Serpentine

WHERE YOU GO: This is a snake-shaped figure *(below)*. **For a three-loop serpentine, begin a circle at *A* or *C*. Half-way around, instead of continuing, head across the ring and begin another half-circle on the other rein. Again, half-way around, straighten up for a few paces before beginning a third half-circle the other way. You finish at the opposite end of the ring from where you began, but heading the same way as before.**

YOUR AIM: To stay organized so you make three even loops, all touching the sides of the ring. Keep your pony bending to the inside of each half-circle, but straighten him across the center.

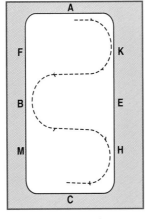

Leg yield

WHERE YOU GO: Start leaving the track at a corner marker. Incline toward the center line. When you are opposite *B* or *E*, start heading back to the track again. A 32-foot (10-m) loop would, at its deepest point, take you to the center line. A 16-foot (5-m) loop is half as deep *(above)*.

YOUR AIM: To make your loop one flowing movement that keeps accurately to the markers. To prepare your pony for each change in bend and get him bending his body through the curves.

Changing the rein

DURING the lesson, the instructor will often ask for a change of rein or direction. There are set ways of changing the rein that make it an easy movement — you don't just stop, about turn, and go in the opposite direction! The first ways you will learn are:

1. Turning across the diagonal *(above, left)*.
2. Turning down the center line *(above, right)*
3. Turning across the center line *(above, right)*.

After changing the rein, always check:

◆ Are you on the correct diagonal? In trot, when you change direction, you must remember to sit an extra beat so you end up still on the correct (outside) diagonal after the change.

◆ Have you moved your whip over (if you carry a whip)? As a general rule, you should always have the whip in your inside hand. Then you can use it behind your inside leg, when necessary, to encourage your pony.

TO move a short whip *(left)* **over, take both reins in your inside hand and draw the whip through with your free hand. Take up both reins again quickly. To move a long whip over, turn your wrist to bring it over the withers. Now turn your other hand to grasp it. Take care with this movement so as not to alarm your pony.**

At the end of the lesson, don't forget to thank your pony with a pat and a few kind words.

THERE are all kinds of exercises that can be done with your pony that will help improve your riding and make you feel more confident and at home in the saddle. Usually, these are done in halt. But if you have a lunge lesson, you may find your instructor asks you to do some of them on the move as your balance gets better.

Exercises like this are fun, but you must always have someone holding the pony. Many of them involve letting go of the reins, and you would not want your pony to walk forward unexpectedly and throw you.

You will find that doing this kind of exercise regularly also makes you more limber and gets your riding muscles in shape, so you don't finish every lesson feeling stiff. You will notice the difference when you can sit deeper in the saddle. You'll be more relaxed about your riding, and you can really help your pony do well instead of getting tense and gripping to stay on.

This is what leads to the stiffness you feel.

Before you begin, you may need to cross your stirrups in front of the saddle and tie a loose knot in your reins to keep them from drooping down.

Mounted

Around the world

First, swing one leg clear of your pony's neck so you are sitting sideways. Now move your rear end around and swing your leg over his rump so you are facing backward. Next, bring your other leg over, so you are facing sideways the other way. Finish by swinging your leg over the neck. Move your legs carefully so you don't startle your pony or lose your balance and slip off.

Ankle circling

Relax those legs. Now circle your ankles around slowly, first clockwise, and then counterclockwise. This will help keep your heels down and toes forward when you get back in the stirrups — without even thinking about it!

Arm folding

Can you fold your arms behind your back? This will help loosen your shoulders and make you sit tall when you are riding.

Arm stretching

Great for getting you sitting deep and tall in the saddle. Hang your legs down low and reach for the sky.

Arm circling

Do this backward or forward, swinging your arms around in large circles. Not too fast! Keep your legs hanging down loosely, and do not lean forward.

exercises

Trunk twisting

Arms straight out at shoulder height. No drooping! Now swing them slowly from side to side. Try to keep your hips in line with your pony's shoulders at all times.

Toe touching

A great exercise for your waist and to get those legs stretching to see just how balanced you are. Make sure your rear end stays in the saddle. Hands out level with your shoulders, then reach alternately right hand to left toe, up, then left hand to right toe. Keep your back straight.

Ankle gripping

Do this one leg at a time — and remember to sit up straight. It is great for loosening the muscle at the front of your thigh. Look ahead, grasp your ankle, and draw your foot back and up.

Touching the ears/tail

Keeping your legs directly under you, lean slowly forward to touch between your pony's ears. Now sit upright again. Then carefully turn to touch his tail.

Leaning back

Face forward, then slowly lean back until you are lying on your pony's back. Now sit up again. Try to keep your legs in the correct position at all times.

ONCE you are feeling secure and confident in trot, you are ready to try a canter. This is where things get exciting! Canter is a rhythmic, rocking pace with three beats that you will be able to clearly hear and feel.

Take a look at the sequence of pictures (*below*). The first beat is made as one hind leg comes down. The second comes from the diagonal pair of the other hind leg and its opposite foreleg landing together. The final beat is from the other foreleg — this is called the leading leg. Then there is a brief moment of suspension when all four feet are off the ground, before the sequence starts again.

CANTER needs quite a bit of extra energy, and getting from trot into canter is a transition that many riders find difficult at first. Usually, this is because they have not managed to get their pony trotting actively enough before they ask him to canter, so he does not have the extra "oomph" that he needs. Or sometimes, the rider is trying so hard to urge her pony on, she slips out of position and the pony gets confused and unbalanced.

Transition: from trot to canter

1 PREPARE to canter by getting the most energetic, balanced trot you can. Shorten the reins and tighten your rear end and leg muscles so he knows something is about to happen.

2 SIT to the trot. Now, staying as upright as you can and keeping a good contact on the pony's mouth, nudge with your inside leg on the girth. At the same time, move your outside leg slightly behind the girth.

3 THE pony's first step of canter is called the strike off. You will know when this happens because it feels like a little spring forward. Keep your contact constant, but allow your hands to move with the pony's head. Although ponies usually enjoy cantering, some can be pretty hard to persuade to move up a gear. Be organized and determined. Sit up with your reins short enough. Get some bounce in that trot! Choose a location from where you are going to ask (going into a corner is best), and use a firm nudge with your inside heel — staying upright. Be ready to use your whip, just behind your inside leg, if the pony does not respond right away.

The canter

TIP

IF your pony does not canter when you ask, don't let him continue trotting faster and faster. Settle back down to a good, active trot. Then, try again.

TIP

UNTIL you are more experienced, it is always best to ask for your canter from a position in a corner or on a large circle. This helps your pony keep himself in balance and encourages him to strike-off on the correct leading leg.

THIS rider will be exhausted before her pony gets the message to canter. "Loopy" reins and the rider's weight tipped forward result in the pony being entirely on his front end. The situation is far too unbalanced to manage a canter strike-off.

WHOA! The rider is so tense and hanging on so tightly that this pony will just keep trotting faster and never actually canter. She needs to lower and ease off the reins, bring her lower legs back, settle into a relaxed trot, and ask again.

Think about your position

AS your pony starts to canter, sit as straight as you can with your rear end down in the saddle. Imagine you are stuck there with glue, and all the back-and-forth rocking of the canter is being absorbed by your hips going backward and forward with the movement. Of course, they can only do this if your body is relaxed, so try not to stiffen up.

Your hands stay level and with a good contact. Don't hang onto the reins for dear life or your pony will wonder whether you really want canter or whether you want him to go back down to trot again. Relax your arms and wrists and let your hands follow the movement of the pony's head, keeping an even contact all the time.

Keep your legs directly underneath you, snug around the pony's sides, but not clinging on. From here, they are in a good position to give an extra leg aid if you sense your pony is thinking about falling back into trot before you want him to. Your legs must be relaxed, too, to keep your knees from tensing and your heels from creeping up.

The Canter

THE world seems to pass by much faster in canter than in trot, so you do have to think quickly about where you are going and what you are doing. But the good news is that it is a much smoother movement, like sitting on a rocking-horse. The extra speed may make you tense and make you bounce around in the saddle at first. But, as you learn to relax and keep upright, you will be able to sit in the saddle throughout the movement and really enjoy the feeling.

TIP

ALTHOUGH some ponies cannot wait to get into canter, quite a few need encouragement to get there and keep going. This is especially true if they are not particularly well balanced, are in a small ring, or are sluggish. Don't urge a slow pony on by leaning forward like a jockey *(above)*. You have the best chance of keeping a good canter all the way around the ring if you keep your shoulders back, sit deep, and keep a good contact on the reins. If you feel the pony slowing — perhaps going into a corner — give him an extra nudge with your inside heel. That's better *(right)*!

OKAY, so you are going much faster in canter than trot, but that is no excuse for riding like a Grand Prix driver, zooming around the corners. Steady your pony by sitting upright and squeezing the reins a little, especially the outside rein, as you approach a corner. Use lots of inside leg. If you let your pony run around the corner, he will get completely out of balance and may slip.

IF you are cantering on a circle or around a bend *(left)*, use the same aids for turning as you would for any pace. Your inside hand asks for the pony to look around the bend, and your inside leg asks him to keep the energy up and bend his body. Your outside hand allows a little so he can look slightly to the inside, and your outside leg stays just behind the girth to keep him from swinging his back end out.

OOPS! This is what happens *(right)* if you tense your leg and grip with your knees. If you lose a stirrup, it is best to come down to trot and start again.

IT'S not surprising this pony is hardly cantering when the reins are so long. If the rider shortens the reins and uses her legs, the results will be better.

TIP

AIM for a canter with short, bouncy strides in a one-two-three rhythm. This will keep your pony balanced and give you good control. To get a bouncier canter, nudge your pony with your inside heel in time with each stride. But make sure your reins are short, or he will only go faster and get more disorganized.

From canter to trot

WHEN you want to slow down from canter to trot, sit tall. Stop encouraging your pony on with your legs, but still keep them close to his sides, directly under your body. Brace your back and press down with your rear end into the saddle. Put pressure on the reins until you feel him slow and break into trot. Then ease off but keep your contact. Remember to sit for a few beats of the trot, after your transition, to help you get organized.

Make your transition as smooth as possible. Try not to let yourself — and your pony — just fall out of canter into a heap, losing all the energy at once. As you make the downward transition, keep sitting up and encouraging him so he does not think he has finished work for the day.

SO what is meant by getting the "right lead" in canter? Although you may think this is too technical to deal with when you are just beginning to canter, it is important information to know. Unless your pony is cantering on the correct "leading leg" whenever he is going around the ring or in a circle, he will never be balanced. He will not feel comfortable and may even trip.

Sequence

Remember that the three-beat sequence of the canter footfalls ends with one foreleg coming down. It is easy to see why it is called the leading leg because, if you glance down while the pony is cantering, you can see it stretch forward.

Listen to the hoofbeats. You can hear the pony's emphasis on the leading leg — *dah, dah, dah*. This leg takes all the weight by itself as it pushes him forward to the next stride.

If you are cantering along in a straight line, for instance on a trail ride, it does not really matter which of the forelegs is the leading leg. But if you are in a ring or cantering a circle, the leading leg must be the pony's inside foreleg. So, if you are on the right rein, the correct leg is the right foreleg. On the left rein, it is the left one.

Listen for the hoof-beats

The

AS soon as you are cantering, glance down quickly (don't lean!) to check if you are on the correct lead. You will see the leading leg stretch forward with each stride.

After a while, you can tell just by the "feel." Being on the wrong leg actually feels less comfortable.

If you see you are wrong, come back down to trot immediately and get ready to try again. You will not be able to get your pony to change leading legs while he is still cantering — that is, until you are a dressage or show-jumping star!

canter 3

Getting the right lead

HOW can you make sure your pony strikes off so he goes onto the correct leading leg?

1. MAKE A GOOD TRANSITION. Practice your transitions so your pony is prepared with a good, active trot. He should respond to your aids to canter immediately, without getting unbalanced.

2. ALWAYS ASK FOR CANTER IN A CORNER OR ON A CIRCLE *(right)*. As long as he is in balance coming into the bend, this will mean the easiest thing for him to do is begin his canter stride with his outside hind leg — meaning the inside foreleg will correctly become his leading leg.

3. BEND HIS HEAD AND NECK slightly to the inside as you ask. This is hard to remember at first, when there is so much to think about. But as you improve, try it. Flexing the pony to the inside of the curve by squeezing your inside rein as you give the canter aids helps him understand which "bend" and which leg you want.

QUICK QUIZ

Can you tell which of these horses is cantering on the correct lead?

ANSWER: A

YOU are probably looking forward to learning how to jump. You might have a few jitters, however, wondering whether you are going to be able to make your pony go over a fence — and whether you will land in the same place as he does on the other side!

Jumping is a thrilling part of riding. Tackling small fences is nowhere near as difficult as it looks, as long as you have a secure position in the saddle and feel confident and in control of your pony at walk, trot, and canter.

Jumping, like everything else in riding, is about balance. Again, you cannot expect success right away or every time. When you first start, expect to have quite a few jerky jumps and maybe some sticky moments. You might even fall off a few times, although, hopefully, you will slide to the ground

Jumping

and land on your feet without any damage being done. Soon, with the help of your instructor and an experienced pony — and starting with poles on the ground and low, simple obstacles — you will build your confidence. Then you will start enjoying it!

1. The approach

THIS is very important. A pony that approaches the fence with plenty of energy, going straight, and in balance will find it easy to follow through and jump. All you have to worry about is staying steady and letting him continue. But a bad approach makes life difficult and gives him plenty of excuses for saying "no, thanks" or jumping awkwardly. For small jumps, approach either in trot or in canter. Sit as still as you can, but keep your pony going forward in a straight line toward the center of the jump. Be ready to urge him on if you feel him slowing down.

2. The take-off

IN the last stride before the jump, the pony steadies and considers. He brings his hind legs underneath and pushes off, lifting up his front legs. He takes off around the same distance from the fence as it is high. There is no need for you to tell your pony when to take off. As long as he is going forward in balance, he will decide this for himself. He may want to get close to have a good look first. If so, keep your body still but use your legs more strongly. Concentrate on trying to stay in sync with him when he takes off. Always look up. This will keep your body straight. The movement will swing your body forward, so let your hands go forward so the pony can stretch his neck out without getting his mouth pulled. Don't lean forward over his neck too early, or you will make it hard for him to take off.

3. The moment of suspension

THIS is when the horse is in the air. Over low jumps, all four of his legs are off the ground together only for an instant. But as you proceed to bigger jumps, there will be several seconds as the pony goes over. During this time, you need to be squatting in half-seat position close to the pony, and as in balance with him as you can be. Your weight is off his back, and your legs are directly underneath you (see *next page* for more about half-seat position). As his neck stretches out, let your arms reach forward.

4. Landing

THE horse comes down on one of his forelegs first, followed quickly by the other. As this happens, his head and neck come up. This feels bumpy to the rider, and it is easy to get pulled forward or thrown off balance. So keep your lower leg well under you or push it slightly forward. Avoid collapsing onto your pony's neck or leaning your hands on him.

How a pony jumps

WHEN a pony jumps, what he is actually doing is taking an extra-large canter stride, with added "pop" in it, in order to clear whatever is in his way. So if you can canter, you will soon get the feel of jumping small fences. Of course, when it comes to experienced showjumping, that extra-big stride is huge. But even so, it's basically the same action as the one a pony uses when he is going over just a small fence.

5. Recovery

THIS is the first stride taken after landing. Now you can gently sit back down into the saddle and take up more contact with the reins again. Use your legs to keep your pony moving forward. As quickly as you can, get organized because, as you improve, there could be another fence coming up!

NOBODY is expecting you to jump over big fences right away or to instantly sit perfectly throughout a jump. Learning to stay with the pony's movement takes quite a bit of skill and many practice jumps.

Getting into the right position over the jump is crucial because it helps you stay secure and keeps you from interfering with the pony. This gives him the best chance to clear the fence smoothly without hitting it. A good half-seat position also

Jumping 2

makes you look stylish and part of a team with your pony. It means that you can see where you are heading! Before you start to jump, always:

Check that your girth is tight — or you could end

up on the ground before you even reach the jumps.

Shorten your stirrups — stirrups are always raised a few holes for jumping. This makes it easier to get into and hold the half-seat position.

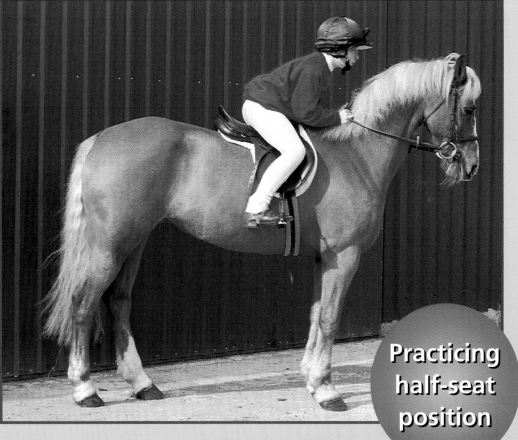

YOU can practice the half-seat position both standing on the ground and on a pony that is standing still. Remember, you should be able to balance perfectly with your feet flat on the ground, or in the stirrups, without toppling forward or backward.

◆ LOOK up and ahead, between the pony's ears.

◆ TRY to flatten your back, sticking your rear end out and your chest down toward the pony's neck so you are hovering just above the saddle seat. Think of your body and legs as a big *W* on its end. What you are trying to do is to squash the *W* as much as you can, so all the angles are closed.

◆ KEEP your lower legs underneath you. Let all your weight sink down through your heels.

Practicing half-seat position

◆ DON'T rest your hands on the pony's neck. When you are balanced, you will be able to move them forward or backward easily.

◆ NOW practice keeping your balance in half-seat position when your pony is moving.

Don't get into a bad position...

YOU can see from these photos why it is worth perfecting your half-seat position, especially as you go on to tackle bigger jumps. All of these ponies are finding it hard to do a nice, rounded jump because their riders are not sitting correctly. Imagine all of the photos with the pony taken out — none of these riders would be able to stay in balance.

Standing in the stirrups

STANDING in the stirrups *(right)* is another common fault. This rider is trying to jump the fence *for* the pony. He has gone out of the saddle too far and too soon, instead of waiting for the pony to come up toward him. Rather than squashing down into half-seat position, he is standing up with straight legs. If this pony had decided to refuse or stumbled on landing, the rider would be too far forward out of balance and would fall off.

Getting left behind

GETTING "left behind" is one of the most common problems and does not happen only with beginners. Instead of going with the pony's forward movement as he takes off, the rider is too far back and gets jolted out of the saddle as the pony's hind legs come up. If this happens, try to slip the reins through your fingers so you don't jab the pony in the mouth. Make sure you are poised in a balanced, slightly forward position as you approach, then squash down into half-seat position as you feel the pony coming up as he takes off.

Looking and leaning down

THIS rider *(above)* is well squashed down. But with all her weight on one side, she is making her pony "flatten" over the jump. Look how his ear is back, thinking "What's she doing?" The chances are he will veer to one side over the fence, or knock it down, and he may well throw her over his shoulder as he lands!

OUCH! *(above)*. Always make allowance with your hands as the pony's neck stretches forward. Otherwise, jumping will not be a very easy or enjoyable experience for him.

THERE are several kinds of exercises that your instructor will use to help improve your jumping technique. Even the very best, most experienced riders use these in their training, especially when teaching a young horse or pony to jump.

Jumping 3

Using Trotting Poles . . .

ONE of the best exercises for ponies and riders is to use a line of poles on the ground, often called trotting poles. This teaches a pony to be coordinated, to pick up his feet, and to get in a nice rhythm. Novice riders can learn to get their balance over the poles before trying a real jump. They can start feeling the kind of regular tempo a pony needs to be doing in order to jump.

The poles are laid on the ground, either singly or in a line, with a set distance in between. You can tackle them in walk at first. Then, when you feel secure and well in control, try the exercise in trot. Your instructor will make sure the poles are always the right distance apart so your pony does not trip over them. For ponies, this is 4-4.5 feet (1.2-1.3 m) apart — slightly more for horses.

ALWAYS approach in a straight line, aiming for the center of the poles. Take your weight slightly off the saddle as you approach, although you do not need to fold down into half-seat position. Remember to look ahead, keep a good contact on the reins, and use your legs to keep asking the pony to go forward.

TRY to stay in a good position over the poles. You may feel the pony slowing up, so squeeze him on with your legs, trying not to lose your balance as you do this. You will feel the bounce-bounce-bounce as your pony picks his feet up higher. It will jolt, so this is when you need to absorb the movement in your ankles, knees, and hips — a bit like you do in posting trot. But instead of going up and down in the saddle, you are hovering in balance just over it.

This rider's pony (below, left) is trotting on nicely through the poles. The rider's weight could be a little more forward with her rear end just out of the saddle.

YOU will probably feel the pony wanting to stretch his neck out a bit more than in ordinary trot, so let him do this by allowing your hands forward. Do not fall onto his neck, though, or give the reins away because you need them to help him stay balanced. If you feel yourself getting unsteady, don't grab the reins and hurt the pony's mouth. Grab the neckstrap or a chunk of mane.

ONCE you are feeling organized over trotting poles, it's time for some real jumping. Your instructor will probably first add a small jump — such as a crosspole — to the end of the line of poles on the ground. The good thing about this is that the poles leading up to the jump make sure your pony is in exactly the right spot to take off when he gets there. All you need to concentrate on is keeping a balanced position over the poles, looking up, and encouraging your pony to stay in an active, forward rhythm all the way. Remember not to go forward before your pony actually takes off. Also, remember to allow a little with your hands as he goes over. Don't let him waver to the side — head straight for the center of the jump.

Starting Gridwork

THE exercise on this page — poles leading to a single jump — is a very simple form of grid. Gridwork is any jumping exercise involving different combinations of poles on the ground and low jumps set in a line. It is very good for ponies and riders because it helps riders keep position and rhythm through the line. It is fun and confidence-boosting for everyone because the poles and jumps are arranged at set distances. This puts the pony in exactly the right place as he goes along, making it easy for him to keep going onward and easy for you to stay in balance with him.

The rider is using her legs to encourage her pony through the poles to the first crosspole of the grid. See how she is looking ahead to where she is going?

The rider could fold forward a bit more to allow her pony a little more rein over the first fence.

Her pony lands in canter and is happy to carry on through the grid. Now the rider sits up with a good contact, to help rebalance him over the next pole.

The final fence in this grid is a small oxer. The pony jumps out well but would have appreciated some more freedom to stretch his neck. The rider should have brought her hands forward instead of resting them on his crest.

POLES on the ground in front of a jump make things simpler for a rider. They put the pony on just the right stride to take off in a good place in front of the jump. As you get better, you will have to learn how to tackle a jump on its own, without a trotting pole in front.

Jumping 4

TIP

ALWAYS come around in a wide circle or arc toward a line of poles or a fence to help keep your pony balanced. Otherwise, he either will not have enough "go" or will start to rush his fences.

Tackling Bigger Fences

It is important as you approach the fence that your pony is:

GOING ACTIVELY FORWARD — You need a bouncy, but controlled, trot or canter *(above)*.

GOING STRAIGHT — Come around in a wide arc, looking toward the fence. Then head toward the fence in a straight line, aiming for the center.

LOOKING UP — Eyes up over the fence, not down!

SITTING STILL AND IN BALANCE — Keep encouraging the pony forward with your legs, but, otherwise, try to be as still as you can. Nothing discourages a pony to the idea of jumping quicker than a rider who keeps shifting around or pulling his mouth as he approaches the fence.

TIP

IF you are approaching in canter, make sure you are on the correct lead leg before coming around toward the jump. This will help the pony get a balanced approach. Look where you are going because it helps you plan a good route and turns your body slightly, too.

Positive Thinking

HAVING a disorganized approach to a fence is not good.

If, by the time you reach the jump, your pony is out of control or totally off balance, the result is almost guaranteed to be either a refusal or a run-out to the side.

Even if he is willing to take off, chances are the pony will probably jump awkwardly and knock the fence down.

MOST ponies enjoy jumping as long as their riders make it easy and comfortable for them. Some can be lazy or uncooperative, so following another more willing pony will usually encourage a reluctant jumper. But most of all, whether a pony will jump or not is up to you.

Always be positive and determined about jumping, even when the fences are very low. If you are not sure, your pony will sense this, and the chances are he will decide not to bother. As you approach a line of poles or a fence, think about your position and get your pony moving purposefully.

We are not talking about going fast — just with plenty of bounce and energy (called impulsion). That requires lots of leg and a good feel on the reins. Don't leave the reins flapping loose for the pony to choose his own speed or to run out to one side. Be determined that you are going to get over that jump. Be ready to use more leg or the whip if you suspect your pony is having second thoughts.

AS you become more experienced and confident, your instructor will soon have you following one fence with another. Before you know it, you will be doing a series of jumps in a course.

Jumping 5

Tackling more than one fence

WHEN one jump comes after another, you need to have your wits about you. Think ahead so you can give your pony good preparation for each one, not just the first. As soon as you land over one fence, you need to recover quickly, organize yourself again, and set your pony up for the next one. Each time, remember all the points for a good approach. Carefully tackle each fence as it comes.

Upright to start

THERE are lots of different styles of fences, but all belong to two basic types. The first type you will jump is called a vertical *(below)*. Verticals are set up on a single set of jump standers. Verticals have no depth, just height. The pony jumps up and over.

Putting on the style

Taking on oxers

AS you progress, you will start jumping oxers, too. An oxer fence has some depth to it, so the pony must not only jump up, but stretch out as well, to clear it. It is usually built on two sets of jump standers, one directly behind the other.

At the double

TWO fences set very close together are called an "in and out." They are always placed a certain distance apart, so your pony should take either one or two strides between them. When you progress to jumping a course that includes an in and out, you will learn how to pace the distance on foot to check how many strides there are between each fence (called each element). With practice, you will soon be flying high with your pony. You may even get the chance to show off your skills at a show *(right)*.

Picking

IF you thought canter was fast and exciting, you will love galloping. Gallop is the horse's fastest pace, the one you see racehorses using as they thunder around the track.

Your pony will not travel at quite that speed, but he still moves pretty quickly in gallop. You must feel safe and secure in canter before you ask him to move any faster. Also, you need to be sure your "brakes" are working and that you stay in balance and control all the time.

Choosing a location

There is not enough room to gallop in a ring, so you will be able to try it only out on a trail. Even so, do not try a gallop just any place. Choose a place where the ground is

Transition: Canter to gallop

WHEN you go from canter to gallop, you will not feel a sudden change of pace or tempo as you do with the other upward transitions. Once you feel you have a good canter, just ease the reins a little, use your legs more, and come forward slightly with your weight out of the saddle as if you were in half-seat position. Now you will feel your pony start to pick up more speed. Listen for his hoof-beats. When the 1-2-3 footfalls of canter turn to a faster 1-2-3-4, and your pony seems to be stretching out to take longer strides, then you know you are galloping.

... and from gallop to canter

WHEN you want to slow down, sit down in the saddle. With your legs well underneath you, put pressure on the reins, then release it. Then "feel" on the reins again and release them. Use this give-and-take action to slow the pony. If you pull continuously and he is happy to keep going, he will take hold of the bit in his mouth and pull back against you.

up speed

The buzz of the gallop!

level and firm and where you know you will be able to stop the pony safely. Remember that ponies cantering together often get excited and start racing, so it is best to practice your first gallops on your own.

In gallop, if you were to stay sitting down in the saddle as you do when cantering, it would be hard work for the pony. This is because his entire center of balance shifts forward when he is galloping.

Keeping balanced

Your aim is always to stay directly over your pony's center of balance. Taking up a more forward seat allows him to stay balanced and use his hindquarters to go faster.

It is best to shorten your stirrups beforehand, which helps you get into a steady forward position more easily. Keeping your reins short so

you can feel the pony's mouth, bring your upper body toward his neck, as in jumping. Your lower legs should stay directly under you, with all your weight pushing down through the heels. Then your legs and body can absorb the movement.

Don't forget to look up!

Staying forward

Look how the pony's outline lengthens in gallop as he stretches out to reach top speed *(below and opposite)*.

Staying forward helps him use his hindquarters and stay in balance.

Pick somewhere safe and level to gallop, and try the feel of it on your own before you pick up speed with others around.

If you feel your pony getting too excited, sit up and steady him right away.

Fun &

WITH a bit of luck, you will have an instructor who makes learning to ride fun. She might think of ways to brighten your lessons with games and other exercises. This will ease tension and improve your riding skills at the same time.

Perhaps you have seen games played at a horse show. Games are great for your balance and confidence. Ponies love them, too. If your instructor has not already thought of it, ask her if you can play some. If you have a pony of your own, get together with a few friends and horse around!

TIP

BY all means, have a good time, but never get carried away and start being rough with your pony. If your pony is lagging behind, don't abuse him in any way. Think about your riding and how to get him moving along more speedily. Be careful not to yank on the reins. Your voice can get the pony's attention, but don't shout!

Ways to play

1 Egg & spoon

THIS is similar to a sack race, except that you have to carry an egg on a spoon (or use other items, *above*) while leading your pony or riding! If you drop the egg, you have to pick it up before you can continue.

TIP DON'T drag your pony along behind you or let him rush off ahead, or you are sure to drop the egg. Try to run just alongside the pony's shoulder.

2 Flag race

(Left) RIDE as fast as you can to the end of the ring and pick up a flag from the holder there. Now, whiz back to the other end, and put it carefully into the holder there. Repeat this until all the flags have been collected and safely delivered. Then zoom across the finish line.

TIP SLOW down as you approach the holder, or you will find that you overshoot or cannot get the flag in it. It is easier if you lean down.

games

3 Potato race

RACE to the end of the ring, dismount, pick up a potato, get back on, and whiz back again, putting the potato into a bucket at the other end *(right)*. Ride around the bucket. Continue until you have transferred all the potatoes, one at a time. If you drop a potato, you will need to dismount and pick it up.

TIP WAIT until you are right alongside the bucket, then lean down to put the potato in rather than dropping it, or it might bounce out again.

4 Sack race

RIDE to the end of the ring, dismount, clamber into a sack, and return to the other end of the ring as fast as you can *(below)*. Sometimes the pony is left for someone else to hold, but experienced riders can lead the pony as they go.

5 Bending race

WEAVE your way in and out down a line of poles or markers and back again to the start. The first pony and rider to finish win, but they must not have knocked over or missed any markers.

TIP KEEP as close to the poles as you can to save time. At the end of the line, make a tight turn rather than going out of the way.

6 Chase me Charlie

THIS is not actually a race, but it is still a popular game for more experienced riders. Riders follow each other over two small fences *(below)*, one on each side of the ring. If you knock one down, or your pony refuses, you are out. After everyone has tried, both fences are raised one hole. The rider who jumps over the highest fence wins. There is another form of this game called Follow Me Fred. Each time around, the fence gets narrower and narrower!

TIP HOLD the sack above your knees and look up, and you will be less likely to trip. Practice getting into the sack lightning fast!

TIP REMEMBER all you have learned about a good approach to each jump, so your pony will jump clear. Don't crowd up to the rider in front, or your pony will not see the jump in time.

NOW that you have mastered the basics of controlling your pony at all paces, you can begin to enjoy yourself, taking him into the countryside on a trail ride. The first trails you go on will probably be with your instructor in a small group. If you have a pony of your own, it is still best to ride with a friend or two, rather than on your own, for safety.

You can explore all kinds of places that cars cannot go, and trail rides can be great fun. You will find it different from riding in the ring in many ways. Your pony is much livelier and more responsive, and you never know quite what is going to happen. A bird might fly out of a tree and startle him, for instance. So you have to anticipate possible problems and react quickly if your pony makes an unexpected move. If your pony does start to get excited or fidgety riding in a group, try to relax and calm him down. Slow to a walk and ask the other riders not to crowd in close. Always keep a safe distance between ponies, wherever you are riding.

BEFORE YOU GO ...

◆ **TELL someone where you are heading and when you expect to be back.**
◆ **TAKE some change for a phone call, or bring a cell phone.**
◆ **IF it is going to be quite a long ride, it is worth taking a small saddlebag or backpack with a first-aid kit, hoof pick, baling twine for emergency tack repairs, spare rein and stirrup leather, and reflective gear.**
◆ **WEAR the right clothing for the weather conditions.**
◆ **CHECK the weather before you go. It is not a good idea to set out as the light fades or in poor weather.**

Opening and closing gates

GATES are often too heavy or stiff to be opened from the back of a pony, in which case you will need to dismount. But it is still important to know how to get through without dismounting. Here's how:

1 WALK up to the gate quietly, and position your pony alongside it so you can easily reach down to the latch. Put both reins in one hand, keeping them short. Undo the latch and push the gate away from you.

2 IF you can, keep hold of the gate as you walk forward, pushing it as you go. Then use your inside leg behind the girth to ask the pony to move his hindquarters around but keep his forelegs still. If you cannot hold onto the gate, make sure the gap is wide enough before you move through, and that it is not going to swing back on you.

3 NOW your pony should be positioned facing or alongside the gate on the other side. Ask him to walk slowly forward to push the gate shut. If you let go of the gate, make sure it does not rebound into your pony. Remember to always fasten gates properly.

Crossing water

YOU might encounter a stream on your trail ride that needs to be crossed. Some ponies are nervous around water and need encouragement to step in, but many love the water. In fact, some love it so much they like getting down to roll. So if your pony starts to paw at the water, urge him forward quickly! Never ride into a deep or fast-flowing river.

In the woods

THERE are a few hazards to watch for when you are riding in woodlands. Rabbit holes could trap a pony's foot. Fallen logs on the ground could make him stumble.

So always check the ground ahead before trotting or cantering. Low branches are another hazard — so be ready to duck! If you come across a log that seems like it could be jumped, look before you leap. Go to the other side to make sure the landing is safe before you jump.

Uphill task

WHEN riding up a hill or incline, lean forward *(below)* with your weight slightly out of the saddle to

help your pony use his hindquarters freely. Look up, and don't let your legs slip back. Allow your hands forward, but keep a light contact on the reins.

All downhill

ON downhill stretches , you can help your pony balance himself by leaning slightly backward *(below)*. Don't lean all the way back unless the drop is very steep. Give your pony a little rein, but don't let the reins sag.

Cross

IF you have ever watched riders tackling enormous fences at three-day events, you probably cannot wait to try some cross-country jumping! It may take many, many years of training before a horse and rider can face mind-boggling obstacles like that. But, if you enjoy jumping and are confident about it, then you will get a real thrill from even some simple cross-country fences. Unlike showjumps, which are usually made of brightly painted poles and fillers, cross-country jumps are all-natural obstacles — logs or walls, or rustic fences made of natural materials, such as timber or brush. Another difference between the two events is that cross-country fences are solid and fixed — they don't knock down. That means that although you will

BECAUSE you are riding a cross-country course outdoors, you can go at a faster canter than you normally would when showjumping in a ring. Between the fences, take a forward position off the pony's back, as in gallop. But as you come toward a fence, sit more upright again and steady your pony to balance and prepare him. When you are doing cross-country, you need to get your pony going in a fast, energetic canter. But never let him dash headlong at a fence. Steady before each obstacle to give the pony a chance to see what is coming up.

Cross-country gear

YOU will both need some special gear for cross-country:

BODY PROTECTOR: Maybe you already wear a body protector for your riding. If you don't generally wear one, you will need one for cross-country to save on bumps and bruises if you do fall off.

GLOVES: Make sure you are wearing gloves because your pony may pull or the reins may get slippery with sweat.

SURCINGLE: Fasten an extra girth called a surcingle over and around the saddle.

BOOTS: Protect your pony's legs from knocks with brushing boots *(right)*. Many riders wear bright jumpers and match-ing silks on their helmets for cross-country competitions.

-country

be approaching the fences faster than in showjumping, you have to be just as careful. If your pony does hit something, it would not be the fence that falls down!

Be confident

SOME riders tackle various types of cross-country fences *(below)*. Always ride on determinedly as you approach each fence, especially "spooky" fences such as shiny barrels or the water. If you are confident, you will make your pony brave. If a fence is lower on the far side than it is on the take-off side, sit well back as your pony lands. When a horse cannot see what is on the other side of the fence, he needs to have lots of trust and confidence in his rider. A cross-country course is one of the three phases of a horse trial — a one-day event or, for the real experts, a three-day event. The other phases are dressage and showjumping.

Road

IT would be great if we could ride straight out of the yard onto a track or bridle path without having to worry about dodging the traffic on roads. But, unfortunately, most of us will have to ride on the road at times.

Many drivers are considerate to riders, but you will always come across some who fail to understand that a pony is an animal that needs to be passed slowly and with great care.

So, before you venture onto the road, you need to be in full control of your pony. If possible, travel with an experienced person at first. Never risk taking an inexperienced or nervous pony near traffic because this could be very dangerous.

You will need to be extra-alert, looking and listening for what is coming up in front or from behind. Be ready for anything that might possibly make your pony spook. You also need to study rules of the road that apply to riders, and learn how to give hand signals to tell motorists what you intend to do.

Using hand signals

Always make your hand signals clear and obvious:

TURNING As you approach the turn, check for traffic in front and behind. Hold your arm out straight, level with your shoulder *(left)*. Keep looking and listening. Do not make a turn unless the road is completely clear. If necessary, stop to wait, then signal again before crossing. Never move to the center and stop there.

STOP, PLEASE There may be times when you need to ask other road users to stop behind you rather than try to go on. Look behind, and turning your body slightly in the saddle so you can see behind you, hold your right hand up *(left)*.

SLOW DOWN, PLEASE If you want a driver who is approaching to slow down, hold your right arm straight out with the palm down. Move it slowly up and down.

THANKS Whenever motorists slow down to pass, or wait for you, always thank them. Then hopefully, they will be just as considerate next time they meet a rider on the road.

safety

Rules of the road

1 RIDE in the same direction as the traffic at the edge of the road. NEVER ride or stop in the center of the road.

2 RIDE in a pair only if the road is wide. At other times, ride in single file. If you are in a group, it is safest to have the most experienced riders and steadiest ponies at the front and rear of the line. If you are riding with friends, remember this is not the time to be chatting and inattentive!

3 YOU can walk or trot steadily on the road, but you must NEVER canter or gallop.

4 DO NOT ride on the pavement in a built-up area, or on any grass dividers.

5 WHEN you want to turn or move out around a parked car, use hand signals well in advance. Keep looking and listening.

Riding at dusk

IT is best not to ride at night because your pony cannot be seen by other road users. When you must ride at night, equip yourself and your pony with reflective gear to reflect car headlights. The rider should wear a fluorescent reflective vest or cross-belt. The pony should wear reflective leg bands. Remember — be seen, and be safe!

TIP

EVEN the most sensible of ponies might spook. Be ready to react quickly, straightening your pony up and getting back in position. Don't hang onto the reins too tightly. Always carry your whip in your left hand (the one nearest traffic).

Glossary

action — the way a horse or pony moves.

aids — signals given by a rider to communicate with a horse or pony.

balance — the way a horse or pony's and a rider's weight are distributed.

bend — the curve through a horse or pony's body as he is moving around a corner or circle.

bit — the piece of the bridle that is held in the pony's mouth, usually made of metal. The reins are attached to the bit. They are the rider's means of giving hand aids to the pony.

cantle — the back of the saddle.

changing the rein — going around the ring in the opposite direction to the one you were traveling in before.

contact — the link between the pony's mouth and the reins; often described as the "feel" on the reins, or by the amount of "weight" in the reins.

crosspole — a small jump made using two poles set in an X. One end of each is supported on the jump stander, with the other resting on the ground.

dismounting — getting off a horse or pony.

dressage — the execution by a horse or pony of precision movements in response to signals from a rider.

figure eight — movement that is in the shape of the number *8*.

filler — a large board that is used instead of more poles to "fill in" a showjump, underneath the top pole.

forward seat — when the rider positions herself with her weight balanced just out of the saddle, slightly forward. Forward seat is used in cantering, cross-country, galloping, and jumping.

girth — the wide strap that holds a saddle in place under a horse or pony's belly.

gridwork — the sequence of small fences and poles on the ground that is used to train a horse or pony and a rider to jump.

hindquarters — the back half of the horse or pony, behind the saddle.

horse — a large hoofed animal of the Equidae family that is over 14.2 hands high. A hand equals 4 inches (10.2 centimeters).

impulsion — the energy and bounce created by a horse or pony's hindquarters as he moves along.

in and out — two showjumps set closely together that are classed as one obstacle with two elements, or parts. There can be one or two strides of canter or a bounce between each element.

inside hand/leg — the hand or leg on the side of a horse or pony that is nearest the inside of the ring or a circle.

lead leg — the leg of a horse or pony that reaches farthest forward in canter, completing the stride. In canter to the left, the correct lead leg is the near (left) fore. In canter to the right, it is the off (right) fore.

lunge — a long rein that is used in the training of a horse or pony to provide some control of the animal.

mounting — getting on a horse or pony.

near side — the left-hand side of a horse or pony.

Get to know your inside and outside reins (above). The inside rein is toward the center of the ring or the inside of the circle in which you are riding.

diagonal — (1) An imaginary line crossing the ring from one of the corner markers to another corner marker on the far side, passing through X. (2) The pairs of legs used by the horse or pony as he trots.

neckstrap — a long, leather strap that goes around a horse or pony's neck for a novice rider to hold onto for extra security.

outside hand/leg — the hand or leg on the outside when a horse or pony is moving around the ring or a circle.

oxer — a type of jump that has width as well as height. It is made of more than one set of jump standers.

pommel — the front of a saddle.

pony — a large hoofed animal of the Equidae family that is under 14.2 hands high. A hand equals 4 inches (10.2 cm).

posting trot — when a rider lifts her seat out of the saddle with the trot's "up" beat and sits gently back in the saddle for the "down" beat. Posting trot makes the horse or pony's back and the rider's rear end more comfortable during trot.

ring — an enclosed, level arena used for training and exercising horses and ponies. The surface may be grass, sand, or a synthetic material.

ring movements — exercises on a horse or pony that are performed in a ring using set markers. Ring movements are very important in the training of horses, ponies, and riders.

serpentine — a ring movement that takes up the entire length and width of the ring. The movement is in the shape of a snake or the letter *S*.

spook — when a frightened horse or pony moves quickly sideways.

standers — supports that hold up poles or fillers that are used to make showjumps. Standers are usually made of wood or plastic.

stirrup — a metal ring that hangs on a strap from a saddle. It supports a rider's foot.

strike off — the first step that a horse or pony takes in canter.

surcingle — a narrow, stretchy strap that is placed over a saddle in cross-country competitions for extra security.

suspension — when all of a horse or pony's legs are off the ground at the same time. There is a moment of suspension in both trot and canter and when a horse or pony is over the top of a jump.

Ride positively, and you will give your horse or pony confidence when tackling cross-country fences (below).

tack — stable gear or harness equipment, such as a saddle and bridle, used on a horse or pony.

track — the imaginary path around the edge of a ring. The outside track is on the edge, and the inside track is just inside this. The route taken around a course of showjumps is also called a track.

transition — when a horse or pony changes pace. A transition can be upward from walk to trot or downward from canter to trot.

trotting poles — long poles laid flat on the ground, often in a line. They are used to teach horses, ponies, and riders how to jump.

vertical — a type of jump that has height but no extra width. It is made using just one set of jump standers.

For Further Study

Books

A Day at the Races. Harold Roth (Pantheon)

The Formative Years: Raising and Training the Young Horse. Cherry Hill (Breakthrough)

From the Center of the Ring: An Inside View of Horse Competitions. Cherry Hill (Storey)

The History of Horsemanship. Deb Bennett (Amigo)

Horses. Animal Families (series). Hans D. Dossenbach (Gareth Stevens)

Magnificent Horses of the World (series). T. Mícek & H.J. Schrenk (Gareth Stevens)

The Man Who Listens to Horses. Monty Roberts (Random House)

Natural Horse-Man-Ship. Pat Peralli (Western Horseman)

The Saddle Club (series). Bonnie Bryant (Gareth Stevens)

Videos

Basic Maneuvers. (Visual Education Productions)

Horsemanship: Beginner Jumping. (Videoactive)

Horsemanship Skills. (Butler)

Rider Skills. (Visual Education Productions)

Riding and Jumping: Basic Techniques with Bill Steinkraus. (Discovery Trail)

The Science of Riding. (Discovery Trail)

Web Sites

www.assateague.com

www.cowgirls.com/dream/jan/rodeo.htm

www.abdu.ac.uk/~src011/pony.html

www.chr.org/

www.aqha.com/

Index